Making Maple Syrup

Therese McNamara
Art by Joanna Czernichowska

Literacy Consultants
David Booth • Kathleen Corrigan

"We're here!" said Luke and Sophie.

They ran to hug their grandma.

"I'm so happy to see you!" she said.

"Where's Grandpa?" asked Luke.

"He's by the sugar shack,"
said Grandma.

"Let's go see him," said Mom.

"Hello, kids!" said Grandpa.
"Would you like to help me
make maple syrup?"

"Yes, please," said the children.
"What do we do?"

"These buckets are full of tree sap.
Help me put the sap in the tank,"
Grandpa said.

Sophie and Luke helped Grandpa
hold the pail. They poured the sap
into the tank.

"Grandpa, how did you learn
to make maple syrup?" Sophie asked.

"I learned from my grandfather,"
Grandpa said.

Soon the tank was full of sap.

"What happens to the sap now?"
asked Sophie.

"It goes into the sugar shack,"
said Grandpa.

Grandpa pulled a hose out of the shack.

"This hose will get the sap
into the sugar shack," said Grandpa.

Grandpa connected the hose
to the tank.
He pressed a button on the hose.
The sap was sucked up into the hose.
It went inside the sugar shack.

Soon the tank was empty.
Grandpa took out the hose.

"Now the sap is in a machine
inside the sugar shack," he said.
"The machine will boil the sap."

"Why do you boil the sap, Grandpa?"
asked Luke.

"Sap has water in it.
We boil the sap to get rid
of the water," Grandpa replied.
"Then the sap gets thicker.
It becomes syrup."

Grandpa and the children went
inside the shack.
Grandma and Mom
were already there.

"I have bad news," said Grandma.
"The machine is broken."

"Oh no! How will we make
maple syrup?" asked Luke.

"We will boil the sap ourselves,"
said Grandma.
"We will put the sap in a kettle.
Then we will put the kettle
over a fire."

"That's how people used to boil sap,"
said Grandpa.

"How much sap does it take
to make syrup?" asked Sophie.

"It takes a lot of sap!"
said Grandma.

Grandpa started a fire very carefully.
Then he put some sap in the kettle.
He boiled the sap.
Luke and Sophie played
while it boiled.
The sap got thicker and turned into syrup.

"Can we eat some now?" asked Luke.

"The syrup is very hot," said Grandpa.
"We have to cool it down first."

"I bet Mom and Grandma
would like some too," said Sophie.

Grandpa smiled.

"I think we all want some," he said.

Mom and Grandma were inside.
They had a tray of snow.

"What is the snow for?" asked Luke.

"Is it to cool the syrup?"
asked Sophie.

"That's right," said Mom.

Grandma poured some syrup
on the snow.

Grandma took a stick and pressed it into the syrup.

Then she rolled the syrup around the stick.

It was a maple syrup lollipop!

"Here is a sweet treat
for our two helpers," said Grandma.

"Yummy!" said Luke and Sophie.

"And here is a treat for us too!"
said Mom.